FANTASTIC FOOTBALL POEMS

John Foster and Korky Paul

OXFORD
UNIVERSITY PRESS

ACKNOWLEDGEMENTS

Acknowledgements

We are grateful to the authors for permission to include the following poems, all of which are published for the first time in this collection:

Andrew Collett: 'Playing At Home (When Late for School)', copyright © Andrew Collett 2001;
Paul Cookson: 'Wizard with the Ball', 'The Goalie With Expanding Hands', 'Every Game's a Home Game with My Footy Family', and 'COOLSCORIN' MATCHWINNIN' CELEBRATIN' STRIKER!', all copyright© Paul Cookson 2001;
Peter Dixon: 'The World's First Goal', copyright © Peter Dixon 2001;
Mike Johnson: 'Old Golden Boots', copyright © Mike Johnson 2001;
James Kirkup: 'Our Goalie', copyright © James Kirkup 2001;
Tony Langham: 'Sub's Lament', copyright © Tony Langham 2001;
Coral Rumble: 'Gran Fan', copyright © Coral Rumble 2001;
Marian Swinger: 'The Witches Versus Wizards Football Match', copyright © Marian Swinger 2001;
Celia Warren: 'Ten–Nil', copyright © Celia Warren 2001.

Previously published poems:

Tony Bradman: 'The Footballer', copyright © Tony Bradman 1989, from *All Together Now* (Viking Kestrel, 1989), reprinted by permission of The Agency (London) Ltd. All rights reserved and enquiries to The Agency (London) Ltd, 24 Pottery Lane, London, W11 4LZ, Fax: 0207 727 9037;
Jeremy Lloyd: 'Cyril the Centipede', from *Captain Beaky*, © Captain Beaky Music Ltd, 1977, reprinted by permission of Jonathan Rowlands;
Trevor Millum: 'Match of the Year', copyright © Trevor Millum 1997, from *We Was Robbed* (Macmillan, 1997), reprinted by permission of the author;
Brian Moses: 'The Anaconda Wanderers', originally published in *Barking Back at Dogs* (Macmillan, 2000), copyright © Brian Moses 2000, reprinted by permission of the author;
Gareth Owen: 'The Commentator', from *Collected Poems* (Macmillan, 2000), reprinted by permission of the author;
Michael Ratnett: 'Over the Moon', from *Over the Moon* (Hutchinson/Red Fox, 1996), reprinted by permission of The Random House Group Ltd;
Rowena Sommerville: 'Oh, Please', copyright © Rowena Sommerville 1996, first published in *Over the Moon* (Hutchinson/Red Fox, 1996), reprinted by permission of the author.

ISBN-13: 978-0-19-276250-4
ISBN-10: 0-19-276250-8

www.korkypaul.com

For all the players and supporters of Team Phil, Team Philipa, Team Jim and Coach Jim White. K.P. (MANAGER)

Endpapers by Oska Paul, aged 7¾

OXFORD
UNIVERSITY PRESS

Great Clarendon Street, Oxford OX2 6DP
Oxford University Press is a department of the University of Oxford.
It furthers the University's objective of excellence in research, scholarship, and education by publishing worldwide in

Oxford New York

Auckland Cape Town Dar es Salaam Hong Kong Karachi
Kuala Lumpur Madrid Melbourne Mexico City Nairobi
New Delhi Shanghai Taipei Toronto

With offices in

Argentina Austria Brazil Chile Czech Republic France Greece
Guatemala Hungary Italy Japan Poland Portugal Singapore
South Korea Switzerland Thailand Turkey Ukraine Vietnam

Oxford is a registered trade mark of Oxford University Press
in the UK and in certain other countries

This selection and arrangement copyright © John Foster 2001
Illustrations copyright © Korky Paul 2001

The moral rights of the author and illustrator have been asserted
Database right Oxford University Press (maker)

First published 2001
Reissued with new cover 2007
10 9 8 7 6 5 4 3 2 1

British Library Cataloguing in Publication Data available

ISBN-13: 978-0-19-276349-5 (paperback)
ISBN-10: 0-19-276349-0 (paperback)

Printed in China by Imago

CONTENTS

THE FOOTBALLER

I take the pass
In the crowded
Playground
And kill it
The ball's tamed
By my foot
And goes where
I will it
To go

I take off
Slow, slide round
The tacklers,
Past the skipping
Girls, dodge
The watching teacher,
Whirl on my heel

Tony Bradman

And maybe
I'll take a shot
From here . . .
My view is clear
Through to
The coats we
Use as posts

Draw back
A foot and SHOOT!
Through the hole . . .
GOAL!
The playground
Fades away . . .
This is Wembley
On Cup Final Day

COOL SCORIN' MATCHWINNIN' CELEBRATIN' STRIKER   Paul Cookson

I'm a shirt removin' crowd salutin'
handstandin' happy landin'
rockin' rollin' divin' slidin'
posin' poutin' loud shoutin'
pistol packin' smoke blowin'
flag wavin' kiss throwin'
hipswingin' armwavin'
breakdancin' cool ravin'
shoulder shruggin' team huggin'
hot shootin' rootin' tootin
somersaultin' fence vaultin'
last minute goal grinnin'
shimmy shootin' shin spinnin'
celebratin' cup winnin' STRIKER !

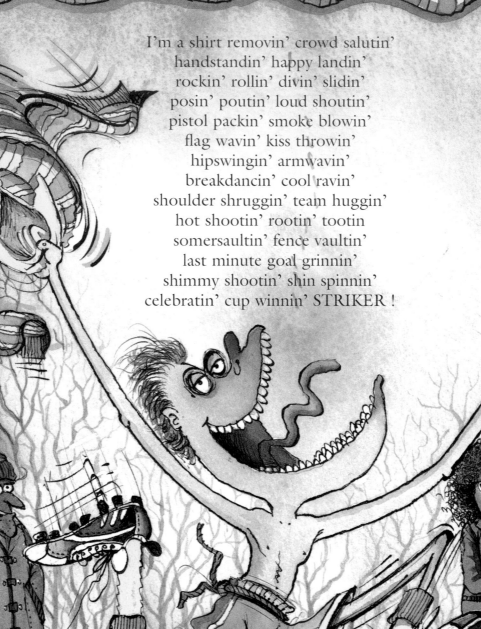

Grandad's in the goal
Dad's in defence
Mother's in midfield
Baby's on the bench

Sister's centre forward
Brother's at the back
Cousin is the coach
Auntie's in attack

Nana is the manager
and just because I missed
a penalty last home match
I'm on the transfer list.

OH, PLEASE . . .

Rowena Sommerville

Oh, please—
let me be in your team,
let mine be the name that you pick,
don't leave me to mope at the edge of the field,
resenting each jump and each kick;

I promise, I'll run like the wind,
I'll twist and I'll turn and I'll pass,
I'll dazzle defenders with sparkle and speed,
you won't see my boots touch the grass;

Or maybe, I'll play at the back,
as solid and strong as a wall,
frustrating all forwards who dare to attempt
the slightest approach with the ball;

But—
each time they play, it's the same,
I'm left on the line, in the cold,
they never allow me to join in the game,
they always say,
'Gran, you're too old!'

I dreamt I played for England
I dreamt I scored each goal,
I dreamt I left the players standing
as I took the team on whole.

I dreamt the fans all cheered
I dreamt they called my name,
before Mum pulled me out of bed
to end my greatest ever game.

TEN-NIL   Celia Warren

The phantom fans are chanting
There's a cheer in my ear as I score:
I've done it again: ten goals to me
And nil to the garage door!

I am delivered to the stadium by chauffeur-driven limousine.
Gran and Grandpa give me a lift in their Mini.

I change into my sparkling clean world-famous designer strip.
I put on my brother's shorts and the T-shirt with tomato ketchup stains.

I give my lightweight professional boots a final shine.
I rub the mud off my trainers.

The coach gives me a final word of encouragement.
Dave, the sports master, tells me to get a move on.

I jog calmly through the tunnel out into the stadium.
I walk nervously on to the windy sports field.

The crowd roars.
Gran and Grandpa shout 'There's our Jimmy!'

JOHN FOSTER ★ KORKY PAUL

10

The captain talks last minute tactics.
'Pass to me or I'll belt you.'

The whistle goes. The well oiled machine goes into action.
Where did the ball go?

I pass it skilfully to our international star, Bernicci.
I kick it away. Luckily, Big Bernard stops it before it goes over the line.

A free kick is awarded to the visiting Premier team.
I'm part of the impregnable defence.
The bloke taking the kick looks six feet tall—and just as wide . . .

I stop the ball with a well-timed leap and head it expertly up the field.
The ball thwacks me on the head.

The crowd shouts my name! 'Jim meee! Jim-meee! Jim-meee!'
Gran says, 'Eee, our Jim's fallen over.'

I don't remember any more.

THE COMMENTATOR

Good afternoon and welcome,
This is Danny Markey your commentator
Welcoming you to this international
Between England and Holland,
Which is being played here this afternoon
At four Florence Terrace.
And the pitch looks in superb condition
As Danny Markey prepares
To kick off for England;
And this capacity crowd roars
As Markey the England captain
Puts England on the attack.
Straight away it's Markey
With a lovely pass to Owen,
Owen back to Markey,
Markey in possession now
Jinking skilfully past the dustbin
And a neat flick inside the cat there,
What a brilliant player this Markey is.
And still only nine years old!
Markey to Beckham,
Beckham to Markey,
Markey is through . . .
No, he's been tackled by the drainpipe;
But he's won the ball back brilliantly
And he's advancing on the Dutch keeper now,
It must be a goal,
He comes off his line
But Markey chips him brilliantly
It's a goal . . .
No.
It's gone into Mrs Spence's next door.
And Markey's going round
To ask for his ball back.
The crowd is silent now.
If he can't get the ball back
It could be the end of this international.

13

And now the door's opening
And yes, it's Mrs Spence,
Mrs Spence has come to the door,
And wait a minute, she's shaking her head,
She is shaking her head,
She is not going to let Markey
Have his ball back.
What is the referee going to do?
Markey looks very dejected here,
He's walking back, hanging his head . . .
What's he doing now?
He seems to be waiting
And my goodness me
He's going back,
Markey is going back for the ball,
What a brilliant and exciting move;
He waited until the front door was closed
And then went back for that lost ball.
He's searching now,
He's searching for that ball
Down there by the compost heap
And wait a minute,
He's found it!
He's found that ball
And that's marvellous news
For the hundred thousand fans gathered here,
Who are showing their appreciation
In no uncertain fashion.
But wait a minute,
The door's opening once more;
It's her, it's Mrs Spence!
And she's waving her fist
And shouting something
But I can't make out what it is.
She's obviously not pleased.

15

And Markey's off
He's running round in circles
Dodging this way and that
With Mrs Spence in hot pursuit,
And he's past her,
What skills this boy has.
But Mr Spence is here too
And Bruce their dog,
Markey is going to have to
Pull out something extra
To get out of this one;
He's only got Mr Spence and the bassett
To beat now. He's running straight at him.
And he's down, he's down on all fours;
What is he doing?
And Oh my goodness
That is brilliant,
That is absolutely brilliant,
He's gone between Spence's legs.
But he's got him,
This rugged tackler has got him,
He's got him by the jacket,
And Bruce is in there too,
Bruce has him by the seat of the pants,
He'll never get out of this one.
But he has,
He has got away;
He wriggled out of his jacket
And left part of his trousers with Bruce;
This boy is absolute dynamite.
He's over the wall, he's clear,
They'll never catch him now,
He's on his bike and
Through the front gate
And I don't think we'll see any more of Markey
Till the coast's clear
And it's safe to come home;
So this is Danny Markey . . .
Handing you back to the studio.

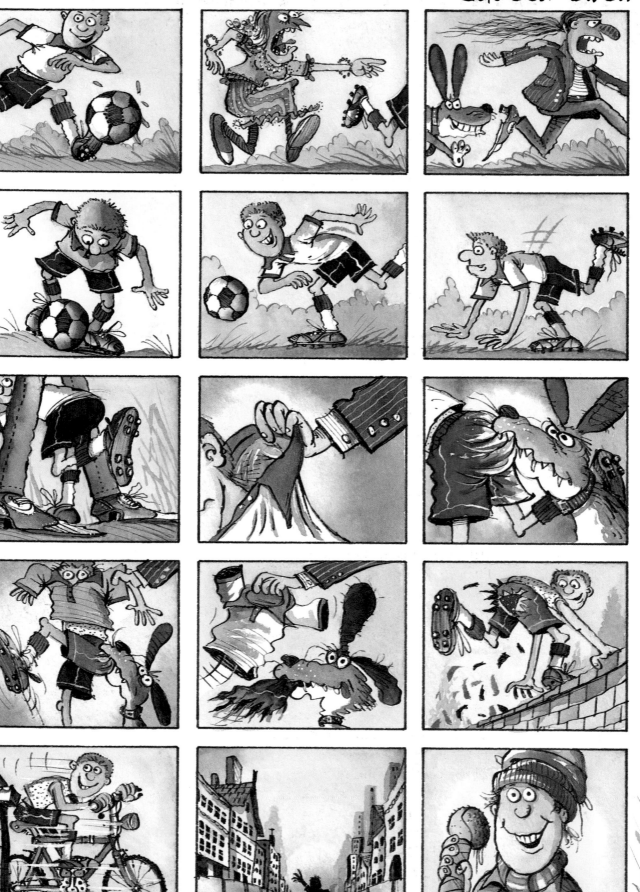

Any crosses, any shots
I will simply stop the lot
I am always in demand . . .
The goalie with expanding hands.

Volleys, blasters, scissor kicks
I am safe between the sticks
All attacks I will withstand . . .
The goalie with expanding hands.

Free kicks or a penalty
No one ever scores past me
Strong and bold and safe I'll stand . . .
The goalie with expanding hands.

18

Let their strikers be immense
I'm the last line of defence
Alert, on duty, all posts manned
The goalie with expanding hands.

Palms as long as arms expand
Thumbs and fingers ready fanned
You may as well shoot in the stand
Not a chance! Understand?
Number one in all the land
Superhuman superspanned
In control and in command
I'm the man I'm the man
The one and only goalie . . . with expanding hands!

CYRIL THE CENTIPEDE

Cyril the Centipede
Loved playing games,
And his favourite one was football.
And when he played goal
With nine fleas and a mole
Nothing got past him at all.
They played spiders and newts
But his hundred boots
Gave his team very little to do
And the fleas would get bored,
The mole never scored
And the crowd would just stand there and boo.
Till one awful day, the crowd stayed away
And no fans for either side came,
But all said and done
When it's none none none none
It's really not much of a game.

Then Cyril the Centipede
Hurt his back leg,
The hundre'th one down on the right.
So he used a small stick
And went 99 click,
Now I'm happy to say it's all right,
But he doesn't play goal
Any more — he's retired
Unbeaten, for nobody scored.
Now he just referees
For the spiders and fleas,
And even the mole
Has just scored.

OVER THE MOON

All over the moon they play football,
All over the moon up in space,
All over the moon every crater and dune,
Boasts a team of an alien race.

Their shirts are the colours of rainbows,
Their skins are a stardusty grey,
And the boots on their toes all have suckers in rows,
There to keep them from floating away.

They play with a meteorite football;
To head it they wear a steel hat,
And the ref's a surprise with his seven green eyes,
But they still say he's blind as a bat.

I watched the Cup Final on Saturnday,
The Allstars played Moonchester Town;
And everyone went, every moongirl and gent,
For the tickets were just half a crown.

And the match that they saw was a wonder,
For both sides had chances galore,
The ball dipped and curled, it was out of this world,
And yet no one seemed able to score.

The ninetieth minute was ending,
It looked like the match was all done —
Then the 'Stars' Number Five smashed a rocketing drive,
A GOAL! And the final was won!

Number Five took the cup from the Moonking,
As the crowd cheered for all they were worth,
And they asked was he pleased with the trophy he squeezed,
And he said, 'Well, I'm over the Earth!'

23

THE ANACONDA WANDERERS

The Anaconda Wanderers
are a wonderful football team.
They strike with such precision,
they're every manager's dream.

They're snaking up the league,
dirty foulers every one,
winding themselves round legs
so the other team can't run.

No one wants to play them,
they are big and slinky and mean.
They threaten to damage the ref
if he favours the opposite team.

Don't hiss or boo or jeer them,
you'd be making foolish mistakes,
you may suddenly find yourself visited
by a gang of angry snakes.

SCOREBOARD

ANACONDA
WANDERERS — 0

SUMMERTOWN
ALL STARS — 6

They're the Anaconda Wanderers,
winning every competition,
slippery in midfield,
tying up the opposition,

keeping them all in knots,
knowing they will defeat them.
And if by chance they shouldn't,
they'll just squeeze them to death . . .
and then eat them!

25

THE WORLD'S FIRST GOAL

In the days of Stone Age people
a long, long time ago
a man invented football
and his name was —
                Stone Age Joe.
Joe made the world's first football
he carved it out of stone
his boots were made of granite
and the goalposts built of bone.

He called his team The Rovers
Joe was their number nine
antlers marked the corners
pebbles laid the lines.

Joe's name is everlasting
for he scored the world's first goal
in a game against United
but it took a dreadful toll.
A cross came from the winger
a chap called Stone Age Ted
brave Joe he rose to meet it
and hit it with his head!
'Gooooooaaaaaaaaaaaaaaaaaalllll . . .'
yelled all the cave folk
'Well done!' cried speedy Ted
but Joe's career was over
for Joe was stone cold
                dead.

They built a grand memorial
to Joe who headed rocks
a football carved of
flint stone
and a pair of
Stone Age socks.

His name will live for ever
upon the players' roll
The Man who started football
and scored the first great goal.

STONE AGE JOE

27

'Off!' screamed the ref.
'Now I've told you before,
no spells are allowed
when the other side scores.
Hurry up now,
change that goalkeeper back
to his usual shape
or you'll get me the sack.
And while you're about it,
that top scoring wizard
doesn't look right
as a footballing lizard.
All those toads over there,
you can change them back too.
The crowd is quite free
to chant slogans and boo.

You can stop all that cackling.
It isn't a joke.'
The ref grew much smaller
and started to croak.
'The ref's gone,'
a wizard cried.
'Have we a spare?
That's the trouble with witches.
They just don't play fair.'
He was changed to a snail
by a witch who sneaked up
and, as usual, the witches
went home with the cup.

Witches Wizards

WIZARD WITH THE BALL

Paul Cookson

Young Arthur Merlin's spellbinding
His skills are crystal clear
A wizard with the ball
He makes it disappear!

And when he makes it reappear
Be sure you can bet
It's resting snugly in the back
Of the opposition's net!

GHOSTLY FOOTBALL

Anon.

As played by the phantoms at Shrule
Midnight football is eerie and cruel,
If one kicks a ghost
Past the other's goalpost
He wins credit for scoring a ghoul.

29

OUR GOALIE

James Kirkup

A raggy pair of gloves for hands,
our snowman stands in the goal.
His eyes are bright green bottle glass,
his teeth are bits of coal.

He has a carrot for a nose
from which an icicle drips.
The buttons down his front are stones,
his ears are my bicycle clips.

He does his best to keep the goal
as we practise taking shots,
but every time he stops a ball
some part of him drops off.

His nose and ears are battered,
and he's lost his big black smile,
so when we shoot the ball, we try
to miss him by half a mile.

Next day, I go back on my bike
to see if he still stands.
— But all that's left is a drift of snow
and the empty gloves of his hands.

SUB'S LAMENT

Tony Langham

Haven't played since they bought me,
When will I get a game?
I'm desperate to get on the pitch.
It's really a crying shame.

Cos I'm just as good as the others,
As skilful as the rest.
All I need is just one chance.
I'm sure I'll pass the test.

I'm as sick as the proverbial parrot,
You probably would be too—
I suppose I'll just have to sit it out.
What else can I do?

Can't demand a transfer.
Can't join another club.
Life really can be miserable,
When you're a Subbuteo sub!

OLD GOLDEN BOOTS

Mike Johnson

Golden Boots 1898

The 'Golden Boot' of Silas Speight
preserved, since eighteen ninety-eight,
when he did something quite amazing;
yes, with this boot at which you're gazing,
Silas scored four times that day.
Trouble though — his team was kicking
quite the other way!

St Ebbe's
SILAS SPEIGHT

SCORE CARD
SILAS SPEIGHT
Phil & Jim 4
St. Ebbe's 0
← 1898 →

GRAN FAN

Coral Rumble

A soccer-mad gran from Dundee
Served her club from breakfast till tea,
She sold programmes and stickers
Knitted team-colour knickers
And crocheted the goal nets for free!